# *Myths & Folk Tales:*

## *Selections from the 2nd International Miyuki Delica Challenge*

*Published by Caravan Beads, Inc.*
*Portland, Maine*

Edited by Barry Kahn
Digital Color Photography by Howell, Ltd.
Printed in the United States of America

FIRST PRINTING: September 2000

ISBN 0-9664319-1-X

Front Cover: "Elvis, in the Guise of a Phoenix, Rises from the Ashes" by Jill S. Cremer

Back Cover:
Top left: "Medusa" by Jennifer Maestre
Top right: "Born and Bred in the Briar Patch" by Julia S. Pretl
Bottom: "The Boy Who Drew Cats" by Judy Walker

Delica® is a registered trademark of Miyuki Shoji Co., Ltd.
Caravan Beads® is a registered trademark of Caravan Beads, Inc.

# Myths & Folk Tales:
## Selections from the 2nd International Miyuki Delica Challenge

## The Artists:

Sequential listing (in the order of the photographs)

1. Jennifer Maestre
2. Mary Tafoya
3. Katherine Meredith
4. Yoshie Marubashi
5. Karen Bruner
6. Linda H. Perry
7. Lisa Niven
8. Celeste Marafino
9. Maggie Meister
10. Nancy Zellers
11. Emlee J. Young
12. Patricia A. Chiovarie
13. Kim Z. Franklin
14. Holley Yeager Bakich
15. Kimberley Price
16. Nancy Eha
17. Noriko Yasui
18. Jessica Fitzgerrel
19. Laura Leonard
20. Debra Smith
21. Kimry Perrone
22. Cindy Bowers
23. Jeanne Dowd Cohen
24. Suzanne Cooper
25. Kathy Seely
26. Margo C. Field
27. Pat Savu
28. Debra Pyeatt
29. Joice Meehan
30. Janet Baty
31. Phyllis Halpern
32. Merna M. Goldetsky
33. Lisa Ring
34. Valorie Harlow
35. Julia S. Pretl
36. Mary Fraser
37. Brenda Ford
38. Robin A. Matthews
39. Bent Needle Barb
40. Jan Zicarelli
41. Shgen George
42. Jacqué Owens
43. Denise Palluck
44. Francis "Casey" Case
45. Kirsten Rugeley
46. Lisa Ann Claver
47. Jean Campbell
48. Suzanne M. M. Warner
49. Jennifer Fain
50. JoAnn Feher
51. Cary Franklin Gasper
52. Stella Broughton
53. Neva L. Wuerfel
54. Marian Crane
55. Nancy Badciong
56. Jill S. Cremer
57. Mary J. Winters-Meyer
58. Delphina
59. Judy Walker
60. Lynn Shansky
61. Amy C. Clarke
62. Maryalice W. Tomoeda
63. Wendy Ford
64. Kerry Smith
65. Bonnie Bousquet-Smith
66. Tacko Matoba
67. Kristin Tescher
68. Marla Kay Shelton
69. Darlene Saric
70. Sue Maguire
71. Linda Karel Sage
72. Susan R. Starkey
73. Keiko Koyama
74. R.A. Hall
75. Toni A. McMahon
76. Marji Brohammer
77. Susan Tucker
78. Jean D. Barstow
79. Brenda Whitehead
80. Patsy Bruton
81. Vivien Exon
82. Tery Baker
83. Christina Manes
84. Mary Lou Allen
85. Elida Cisneros
86. Jennifer Bumann
87. Jane Davis

# The Artists
by last name

# Prizewinners

| | | |
|---|---|---|
| Grand Prize | Linda H. Perry, FL | *Mother Earth (6)* |
| 1st Prize Sculpture | Jill S. Cremer, CA | *Phoenix as Elvis (56)* |
| 1st Prize Body Adornment | Christina Manes, SD | *Farouche (83)* |
| 1st Prize Wall Hanging | Margo C. Field, NM | *Miss Kitty–I love you! (26)* |
| 2nd Prize Sculpture | Laura Leonard, MN | *Baba Yaga (19)* |
| 2nd Prize Body Adornment | Delphina, OK | *Phoenix Rising (58)* |
| 2nd Prize Wall Hanging | Shgen George, AK | *Box of Daylight (41)* |
| Judge's Choice | JoAnn Feher, WA | *The Frog Prince (50)* |
| Judge's Choice | Patricia A. Chiovarie, WA | *Hecate (12)* |
| Judge's Choice | Jennifer Bumann, WI | *Dragon Purse (86)* |

# Finalists

Finalists' entries were in the running for prizes until the final rounds of judging. It is at this stage of the judging that very small differences in originality, perceived difficulty, or other criteria sway the judges toward one entry or another.

| | | |
|---|---|---|
| Kimberley Price | Ontario, Canada | *The Princess and the Pea (15)* |
| Cary F. Gaspar | Illinois | *The Genie of the Lamp (51)* |
| Mary Tafoya | New Mexico | *Medusa (2)* |
| Francis "Casey" Case | Arizona | *Gifts of the Great Creator (44)* |
| Julia S. Pretl | Maryland | *Born and Bred in the Briar Patch (35)* |
| Lisa Ring | California | *Jungle Book (33)* |
| Lynn Shansky | California | *Vasilisa the Wise and Clever (60)* |
| Wendy Ford | Iowa | *The Tortoise and the Hare (63)* |
| Valerie Harlow | Minnesota | *The March Hare (34)* |
| Vivien Exon | Bedford, United Kingdom | *The Black Dragon of Peking (81)* |
| Judy Walker | California | *The Boy Who Drew Cats (59)* |

# Foreword and Acknowledgements

*Barry Kahn*

**Myths and Folk Tales** consists of two parts. The first is this book. The second part can be reached from our website: *www.caravanbeads.com*. (Look for the link titled **2nd Challenge Book**.) There we have provided the artists a place to share the myths and legends which inspired these entries, personal information about their development as bead artists and about the making of their entries, links to their websites if they have them, additional thoughts about the judging process, rules for the **3rd Miyuki Challenge** and more. My initial intent was to publish all of the above in this book, but like over-packing a suitcase, the more I stuffed and crammed, the messier everything looked. In the end, I decided to let the pictures speak for themselves with the text free to occupy as much of cyberspace as it needs.

I would like to thank many people for their assistance:

The artists who sent us their incredible beadwork. I still shake my head in amazed disbelief when I look at these photographs.

Charlene Coutre Steele, Carol Wilcox-Wells, and Diane Fitzgerald, our judges.

Masayoshi Katsuoka, President of Miyuki Shoji Co., Ltd., and his talented employees who make the world's most beautiful little beads.

Carolyn Mitchell and her husband Joe who helped in many small and large ways to prepare for the judging and to host and entertain the judges.

Pamela Clark and the rest of the Caravan Beads staff, past and present, who are always there when I need them and always do more than I ask.

Paul Howell and his staff for their excellent digital photography.

And finally my daughters, Heather and Jocelyn, both of whom helped with the web portion of this project, and other staff members who assisted with the editing.

# Comments from the Judges

*Carol Wilcox-Wells*

It is hard to describe the wonder and awe that I felt as I looked at all of the pieces submitted for the competition. My eyes were drawn to so many beautiful works at one time that I had to step back and try to regain my focus. How was I going to be able to evaluate each piece when I couldn't stop my eyes from wandering?

As I walked around the room that first evening, I was humbled by the creativity of the artists and by the time spent designing, planning, and executing these works of art. To take a theme, Myth, and put your own vision of that out into the world in beads takes courage, and I want to thank all of you who entered.

I also want to thank Barry Kahn for his organizational skills. He arranged the works into their categories, provided us with a notebook portraying each entry and its myth, and he was there to answer any and all of our questions.

To help with the process of judging, Diane Fitzgerald, Charlene Steele, and I came up with seven criteria that each piece had to meet within a scale of 1 to 10. The criteria were: visual presence, craftsmanship, difficulty, use of beads, use of color, originality/creativity, and connection to the myth. Using this process each of us would look at the work and evaluate it. We then shared opinions and decided if the entry was out of the running or should be put to the side for further consideration. I must tell you this was hard work and by the end of each day we were drained, but in a good way. The beadwork in this book is outstanding and as you view it you will understand how hard it was to choose the winners.

*Carol Wilcox-Wells, is the author of **Creative Bead Weaving** and the owner of **Love To Bead**, a mail order and retail bead shop. Her work has been collected and exhibited internationally and she has been featured in numerous publications including **Ornament** and **Lapidary Journal** magazines as well as several books. She is a member of the Southern Highland Craft Guild and resides in Asheville, North Carolina.*

*Diane Fitzgerald*

Imagine there are 147 pieces of beadwork before you. Each is the result of hours of patience, love, and skill. As you examine them, the winners begin to emerge. They draw you to them; they engage your thinking. They are like verbs that communicate action, being, or state of being—not nouns or adjectives that just exist or even exclamations that shout.

Visual presence is what I looked for. It's the power of a work to compel your attention, a masterpiece that stops you in your tracks. A masterpiece—a winner—is about strength of form, about lines that guide your eye in viewing the piece, about texture that makes you want to touch it. But somehow, through all these elements, it's the spirit of the piece that moves you. Somehow the winning piece must speak its message silently, soul to soul, to tell you its secrets.

The piece must hold up under close examination as well. Does the beader use a stitch appropriate for the desired effect? Has she selected beads in colors, sizes and shapes and used them in a way to enhance her vision? Is her work neat? Does the thread color blend or is it used to shift the color of the beads? In beadwork, execution does count.

Fortunately for the judges, many contests have a "Judge's Choice" award so that the personal eccentricities of a judge can be accommodated and she won't be inhibited in making her selection of the strongest piece by her personal taste. For the **2nd Miyuki Delica Challenge**, we agreed on the Grand Prize Winner and the First and Second Place winners in each of the three categories: Body Adornments, Sculpture, and Wall Hangings. But for me, the piece that moved me with its poignancy was the little Frog Prince. He called out, "Kiss me!" as he snuggled in my hand. If he had been larger, I might have ignored him. But there he stood, the gold beads in his belt already slightly worn, beckoning with his little golden mask, suggesting there might be something else behind the mask of red eyes and ugly frog lips. He spoke to me in a way the other entries never would, and I said, "Yes!"

*Diane Fitzgerald is a bead artist who works in a variety of contemporary bead assemblage techniques using seed beads and larger glass beads. Since 1989, Diane has taught a wide range of bead classes at her shop, **Beautiful Beads**, in Minneapolis, Minnesota and around the country. Additionally, her work has appeared in several major exhibits. Diane has traveled to the Czech Republic, Germany, South Africa and other areas to learn about beads and beadwork. Diane is the author of **Beads and Threads: A New Technique for Fiber Jewelry**, (with co-author Helen Banes), **Counted and Charted Patterns for Flat Peyote Stitch**, **Sea Anemone Beadwork**, **Zulu Beaded Chain Techniques**, **More Zulu Beadwork**, and **Beading With Brick Stitch**, to be published in early 2001 by Interweave Press. She also writes for several magazines including **Beadwork, Jewelry Craft, Lapidary Journal**, and others.*

*Charlene Coutre Steele*

When I first stepped into the room containing the entries for the **2nd Miyuki Delica Challenge**, my mouth dropped open and remained that way for several minutes. I was in a "beaded wonderland." To see a room filled with such an amazing variety of colorful pieces was sensory overload. When I was finally able to come to my senses, the only word I could say was, "WOW!"

Judging the **Challenge** proved to be not only fun, but very difficult. It was quite obvious that all contestants put an enormous amount of heart and soul into their work. The thought that went into the chosen myth, the careful selection of color, the variety of beads and stitches used were all taken into consideration when determining the finalists.

While our job as judges was to choose "winners," all of the entries were winners in my book. It is truly wonderful and inspiring to see such an abundance of talent and creativity in our growing community of bead artists.

*With a degree in fine arts and dreams of becoming a painter, Charlene Coutre Steele found work as a commercial artist to be more profitable. She put her design skills to use in the areas of print, multi-media, and video graphics.*

*After 14 years of demanding clients and deadlines, Charlene and her husband Daniel wanted to have their own business. Her love of jewelry design pointed her to an ad in a magazine which led to a phone call to Barry Kahn.*

*Charlene and Daniel were the first licensees of Caravan Beads and opened their store in Chicago in 1994. The business grew and moved to a larger location in 1998. The new store has two classrooms where they offer many classes in beading and also glass beadmaking. Charlene has currently caught the hot glass bug along with Daniel. They are presently collaborating on various fused glass projects in their spare time.*

## Photographs of Selected Entries

The sequence of photographs on the following pages suggested the categories listed below: (the photo numbers follow each category)

1) Women of Power and Influence. (1-26)
2) Egyptian. (27-30)
3) Jewish/Yiddish. (31-32)
4) Literature-based. (33-39)
5) Native American. (40-49)
6) Fairy Tales. (50-52)
7) The Phoenix and Firebird. (53-58)
8) Assorted Folk Tales, Myths and Legends. (59-78)
9) Dragons. (79-87)

The photographs are followed by a listing of the artists, titles of the entries, and brief descriptions of the works and techniques used.

For more information about all aspects of the **2nd Miyuki Delica Challenge**, please visit the electronic portion of this book at *www.caravanbeads.com*.

2

4

6

15

18

24

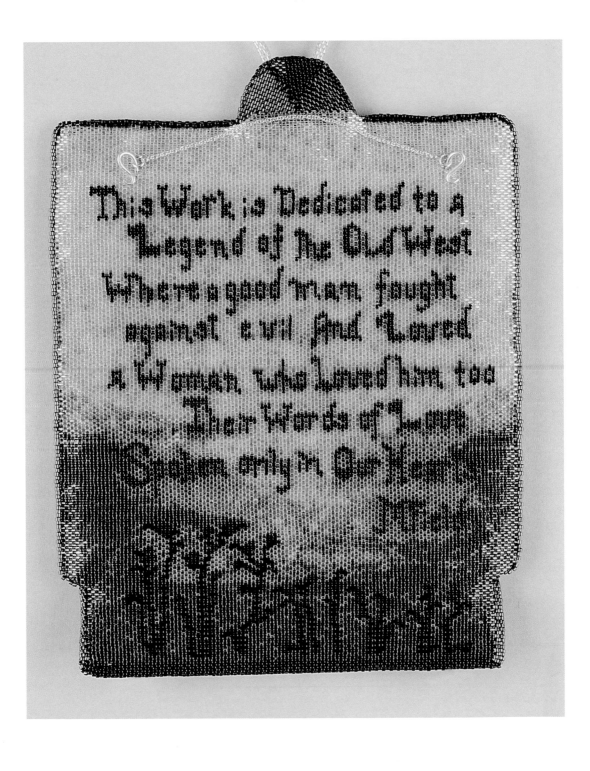

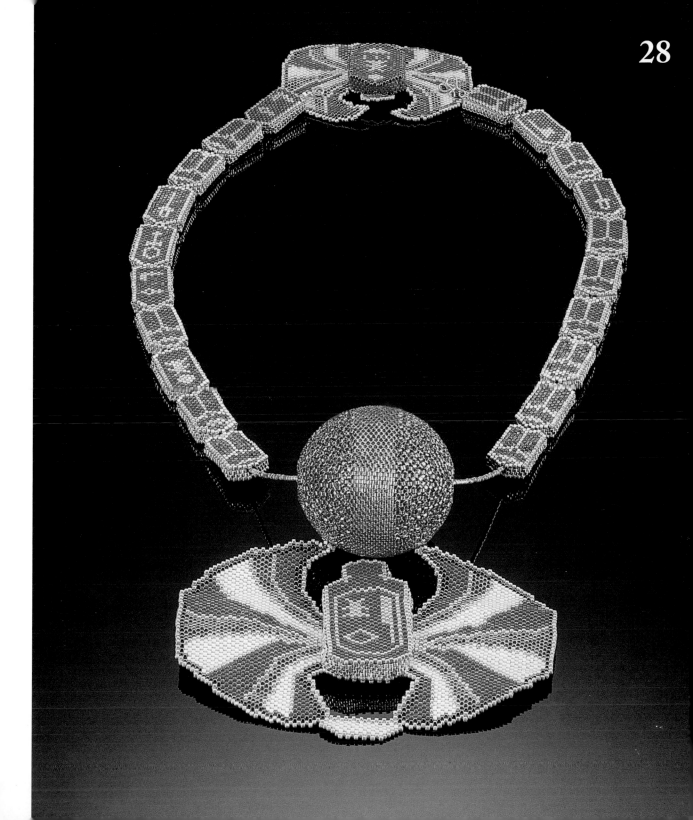

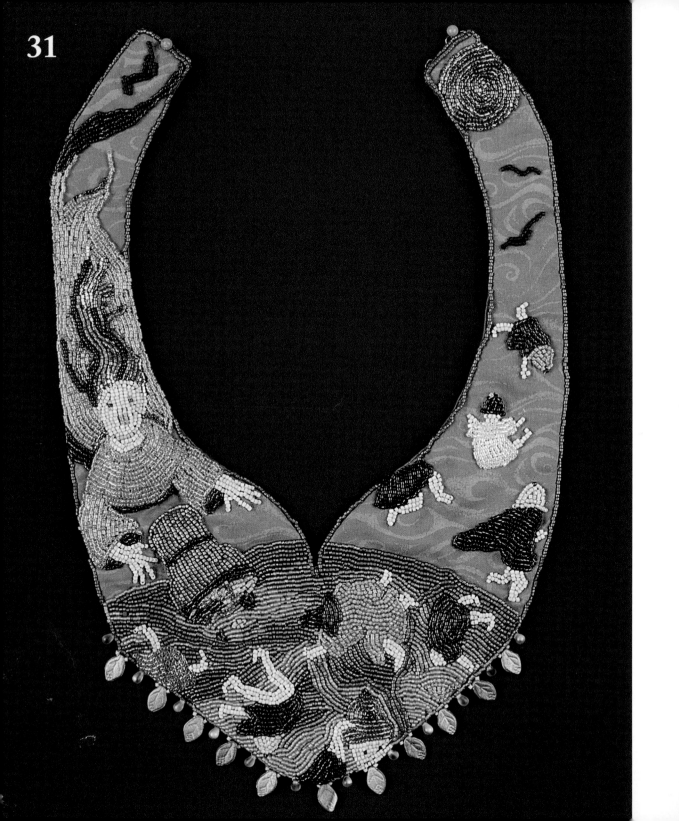

31

33

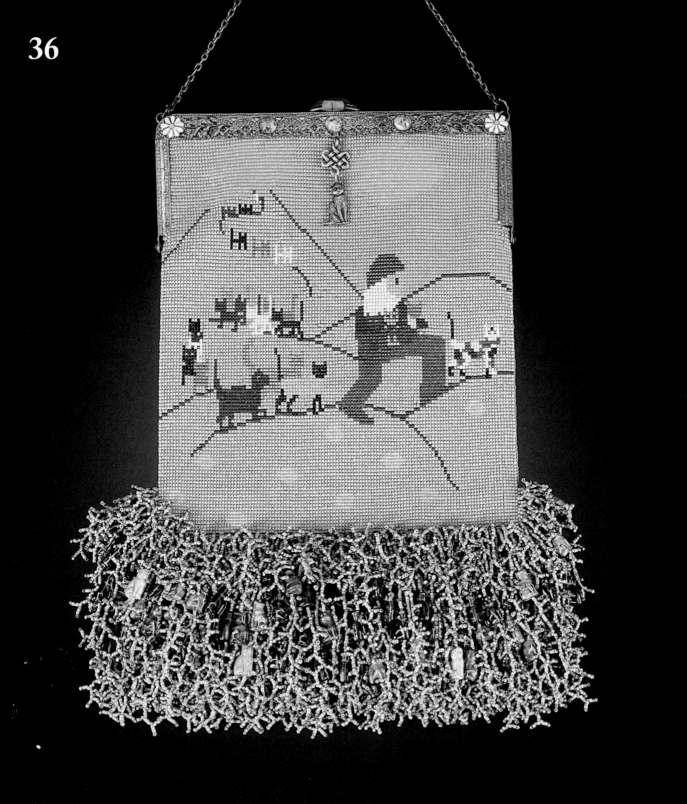

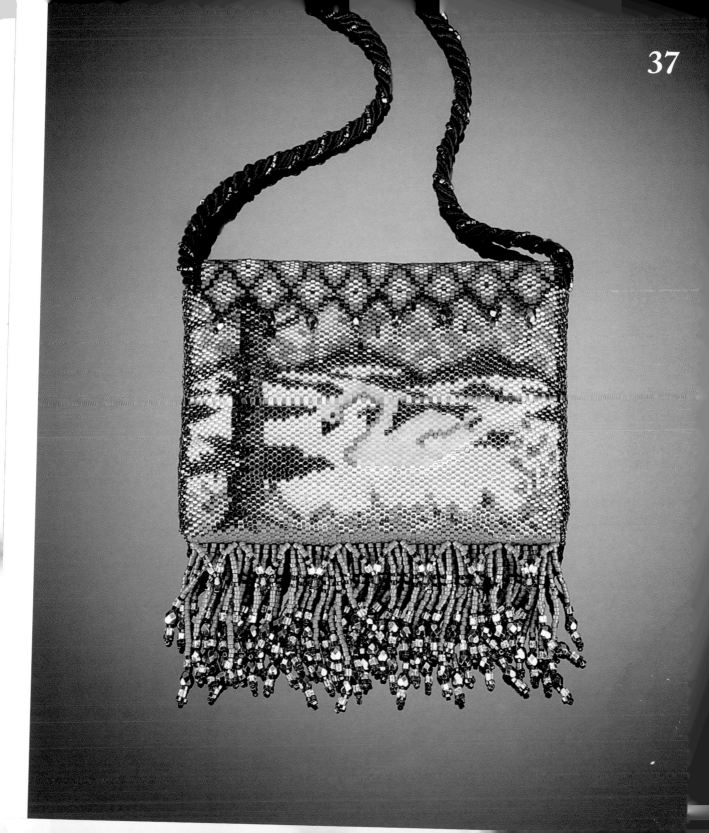

51

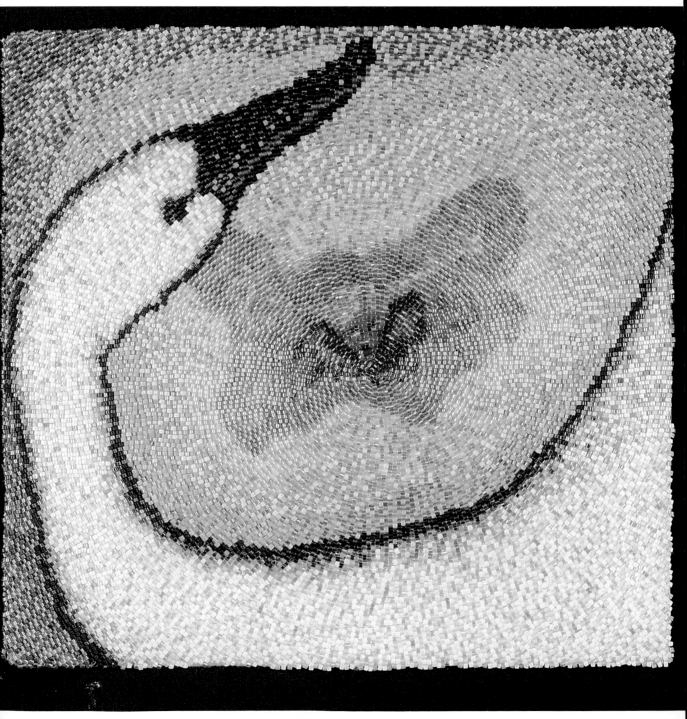

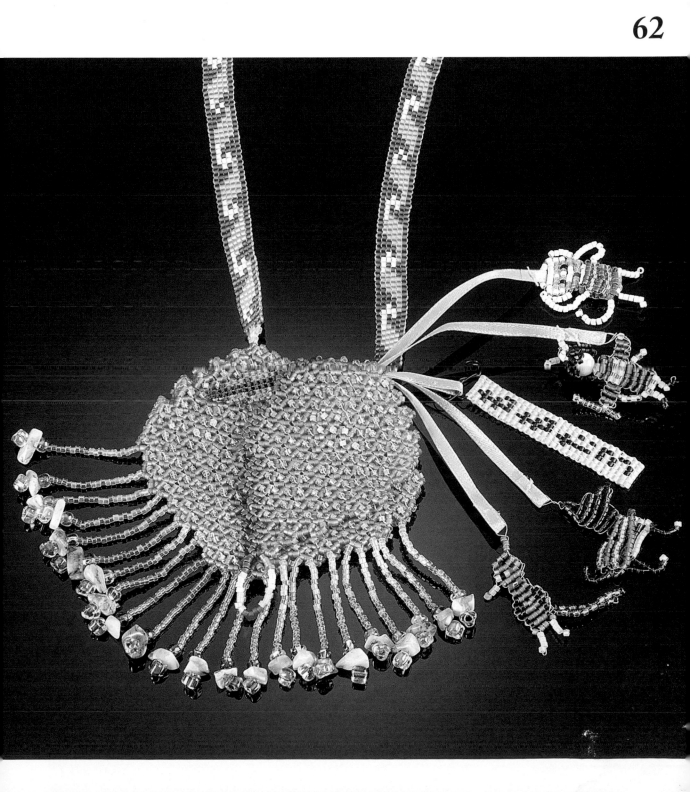

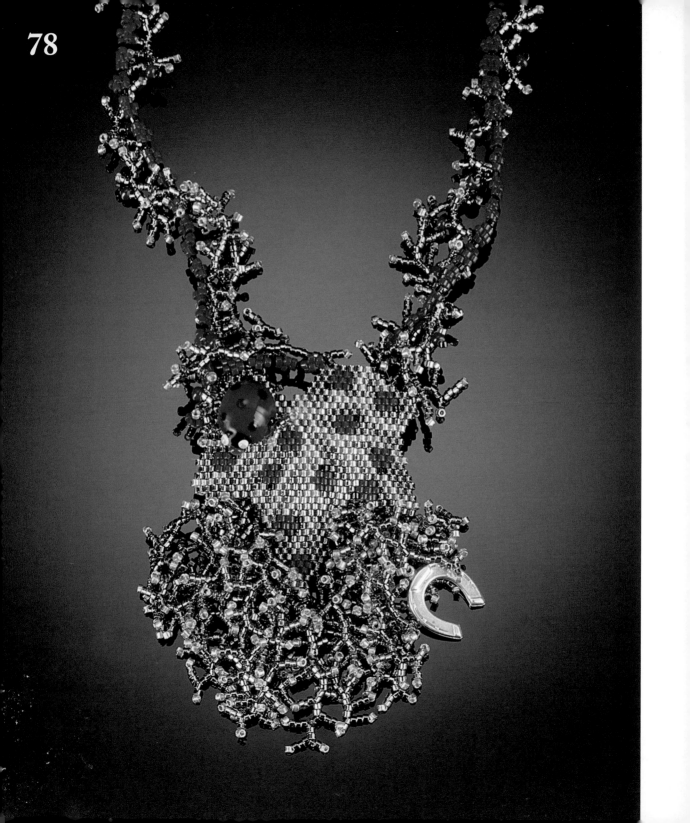

81

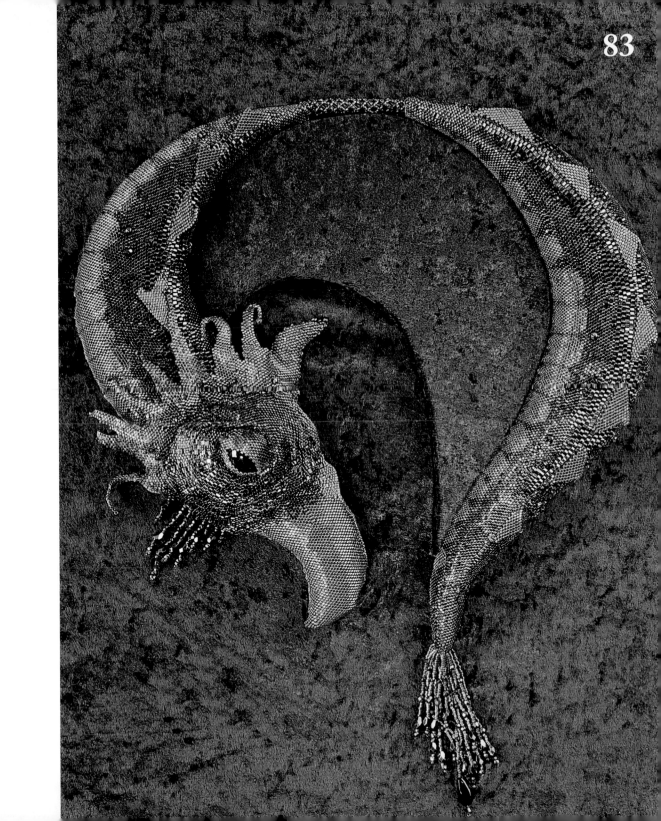

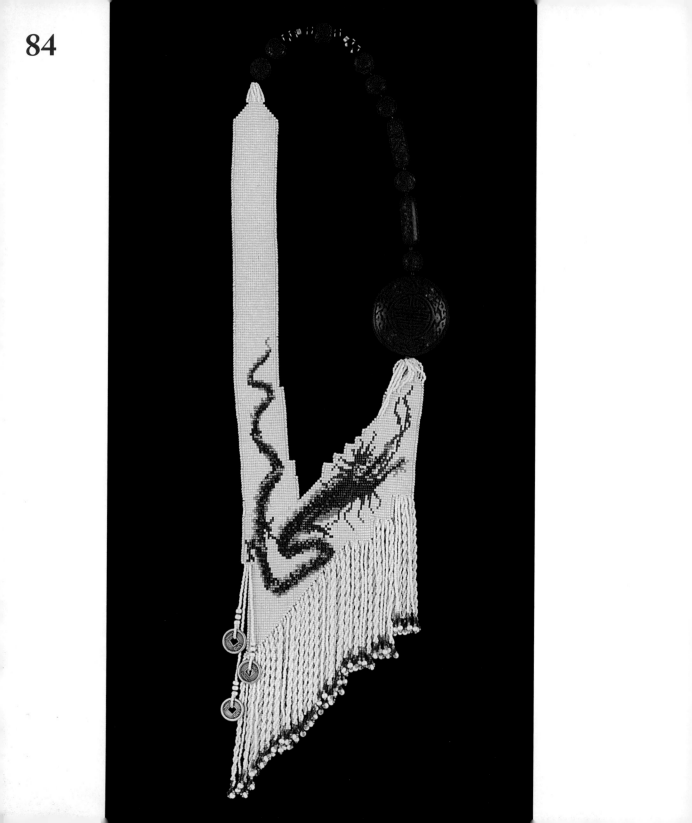

# Women of Power and Influence

*1. Jennifer Maestre*
"Medusa"   15 x 5 x 2 inches
Category: Body Adornment
Amulet bag with snake for lid.
Peyote stitch, brick stitch, right-angle weave, and invented stitch on some of the snakes.

*2. Mary Tafoya*
"Medusa"   9 x 5 x 1 inches
Category: Sculpture
Hand mirror
Trapunto quilting, single needle appliqué, tubular peyote stitch, brick stitch, and simple netting.
Mounted on a custom-made oak mirror.

*3. Katherine Meredith*
"Medusa on a Good Hair Day"   17.5 x 6.5 inches
Category: Body Adornment
Loomwork, random peyote stitch, branched fringe, and surface embellishment.

*4. Yoshie Marubashi*
"Medusa"   7 x 3 x 3 inches
Category: Sculpture
The pouch was created using beads, thick thread, and crochet techniques.

*5. Karen Bruner*
"Medusa"   9 x 2 x 4.5 inches
Category: Sculpture
In-the-round and flat peyote stitch were used.

*6. Linda H. Perry*
"Mother Earth"   15.5 x 8 x 10 inches
Category: Sculpture
Single- and two-drop peyote, single- and multiple-drop brick stitch, plain and erratic square stitch, my own "dragon scale" stitch, horizontal netting, branched fringe, and a lot of WIT (whatever it takes) stitch.

*7. Lisa Niven*
"Gaia"   12 inches
Category: Sculpture
Right-angle weave, peyote stitch (increasing, decreasing, two- and three-drop, and freeform), brick stitch, appliqué stitch, branched fringe, netting stitch, freeform, and coiled wirework. The body is a custom-made doll form created by my friend Judy Walberg. The earth is peyote stitched around a three inch styrofoam ball.

### 8. Celeste Marafino
"Flora"   6 x 4 inches
Category: Sculpture
Tubular and freeform peyote stitch.

### 9. Maggie Meister
"The Siren–Partenope"   11.5 x 6 inches
Category: Wall Hanging
The body of the piece is an original design, graphed and worked in flat peyote stitch. The border, done in square stitch, is from *Celtic Charted Patterns #163*. There is surface embellishment on the wings and 14/0s adorn her hair. A small portion of her body was done in brick stitch to distinguish between the breast of the bird and her wings.

### 10. Nancy Zellers
"A Fragment of the Girdle of Venus"   4 x 12 x .5 inches
Category: Wall Hanging
Flat peyote with decreases form the rose petals and a modified peyote spike technique form the centers. The swan was embroidered in layers for added dimensionality. The cording is a modified African helix. The myrtle is based upon branched fringe. The supportive base was constructed with right-angle weave.

### 11. Emlee J. Young
"The Tooth Faerie"   12 x 12 x 15 inches
Category: Sculpture
Flat, sculpted, and tubular peyote; daisy chain and variations; diamond mesh, box mesh; straight drop-one stitch; leaf stitch and leaf chain; picot lace; and edge stitch.

### 12. Patricia A. Chiovarie
"Hecate"   10 x 6 inches
Category: Sculpture
Beneath the beaded exterior is a form crocheted with cotton thread, supported by wire and stuffed with poly-cotton batting. Techniques include: couching, appliqué, branching, spot-beading, peyote, square, and brick stitching. The three faced head is made of a mirror disc, hand-made polymer clay face, and hand-painted face crocheted together and beaded.

### 13. Kim Z. Franklin
"Eve and the Serpent"   16 x 27 inches
Category: Wall Hanging
Single needle, one-drop peyote stitch with improvisation as needed. The forms of Eve and the serpent were beaded over wire and cotton batting in order to create a modest 3 dimensional effect. Lampworked bead apples and peyote stitched leaves complete the piece.

### 14. Holley Yeager Bakich
"Ameratsu, Goddess of the Sun"   36 x 16.25 inches
Category: Wall Hanging
Beads were sewn directly onto velvet backed by interfacing. In most places, the beads were sewn on in "lazy stitch" fashion, four beads for each stitch. To create smooth curves, however, fewer beads were used. The face is leather, with applied details and set-in doll eyes.

### 15. Kimberley Price
"The Princess and the Pea"   9.5 x 4 x 2 inches
Category: Sculpture
Stitches used include: peyote stitch (one- and two-drop) brick stitch, square stitch, right-angle weave, kinky fringe, 3-strand braid and multi-bead edging.

### 16. Nancy Eha
"The Great Goddess: Child, Maiden, Mother, Crone"   20 x 8.5 inches
Category: Wall Hanging
"The Great Goddess" was hand beaded onto machine-pieced cottons using brick stitch and bead embroidery.

### 17. Noriko Yasui
"Apple: Snow White and the Seven Dwarves"   17.8 x 45 centimeters.
Category: Wall Hanging

### 18. Jessica Fitzgerrel
"Lady of the Lake"   12 inches
Category: Sculpture
The doll was made using a pattern from *Soft Doll and Animals Magazine* called "Pinky, Fairy of Petunia Garden" by Patti Culea that I modified by changing the feet, the head, and the joints at the elbows and knees. The dress is sewn in peyote stitch, and netting pulls the body of the dress, the arm bands, and the edge of the sleeves together. Grass was sewn using increasing and decreasing peyote. Fringes were sewn to make hair; floral wire was added to make some strands stand out. The blade of Excalibur was made with square stitch, the hilt odd count peyote, and the pommel decreasing circular peyote.

### 19. Laura Leonard
"Baba Yaga"   12 x 6 x 10 inches
Category: Sculpture
The piece was made using peyote stitch, right-angle weave, brick stitch, and bead embroidery over a fabric-wrapped armature.

### 20. Debra Smith
"Pandora's Box"   6 x 4 x 3 inches
Category: Sculpture
Peyote and brick stitch were used to make this piece.

### 21. Kimry Perrone
"Dryad Spirit"   5 x 9 inches
Category: Body Adornment
This piece was made using peyote stitch; it was stitched flat and then the two sides were sewn together.

### 22. Cindy Bowers
"Dryad"   5 x 12 inches
Category: Sculpture
Stitches used include: peyote stitch, Ndebele stitch, and branched fringe.

### 23. Jeanne Dowd Cohen
"Brighid the Flame"   16.5 x 8 inches
Category: Wall Hanging
Brighid was created using sculptural peyote and ruffle stitch.

### 24. Suzanne Cooper
"The Wrath of Madame Pele"   6 x 17 inches
Category: Body Adornment
This piece was made using flat peyote with surface embellishment.

### 25. Kathy Seely
"Epona"   10 x 14 inches
Category: Body Adornment
This Celtic collar is executed in a technique that I devised and which I call "flat sculptural peyote stitch." Increases and decreases are used to achieve a predefined shape, the separate pieces were woven and sewn together. The stylized horse and interlace designs are woven into the piece from a drawing. The fossilized horse's tooth was wrapped with peyote stitch and topped with sewn bead embroidery.

### 26. Margo C. Field
"Miss Kitty–I Love You!"   16.5 x 33cm
Category: Wall Hanging
The scene of Miss Kitty and Matt Dillon embracing in the Long Branch Saloon was done in back stitch. The TV frame, control knobs, antennae, and the back of the work are all done in versions of peyote stitch.

# Egyptian

### 27. Pat Savu
"Horus, Lord of the Horizon"   5.25 x 14.5 inches
Category: Body Adornment
This pectoral is done mostly in square stitch. The strap was assembled using single, two-drop and three-drop brick stitch and square stitch.

### 28. Debra Pyeatt
"Tribute to Khepri"   19 x 5 inches
Category: Body Adornment
Flat peyote, circular peyote, brick stitch, right-angle weave, 3-dimensional surface embellishment.

### 29. Joice Meehan
"The Pharaoh"   3.5 x 2.75 inches
Category: Body Adornment
The amulet pouch is done in brick stitch with peyote tube beads for the strap.

### 30. Janet Baty
"Egyptian Goddess"   21 inches
Category: Body Adornment
Circular peyote and straight fringe were used to construct the piece.

# Jewish/Yiddish

### 31. Phyllis Halpern
"Fools of Chelm"   8 x 12 inches
Category: Body Adornment

### 32. Merna M. Goldetsky
"Elijah's Tears"   12 x 7.25 inches
Category: Wall Hanging
The base of the wall hanging is constructed in even count flat peyote stitch.

# Literature-based

### 33. Lisa Ring
"Jungle Book"   6 x 2.5 inches
Category: Body Adornment
The body of the bag was worked in tubular peyote with flat peyote for the sculptured head and ears. The snake consists of flat peyote sections joined to form tubes. The snake head was done in brick stitch, and the branched fringe ends in brick stitch leaves.

**34. Valorie Harlow**
"The March Hare"   6 x 6 x 13 inches
Category: Sculpture
The rabbit's body is made with peyote stitch, the jacket with right-angle weave, and the teapot is peyote stitch with a brick stitch cover.

**35. Julia S. Pretl**
"Born and Bred in the Briar Patch"   12 x 5.5 inches
Category: Body Adornment
Two-bead unfinished square stitch was used to form the choker and the main body, with vertical netting connecting the two. Plain fringe was used for the choker and branched fringe on the briar patch.

**36. Mary Fraser**
"Millions of Cats"   7 x 12 inches
Category: Body Adornment
This piece was created using square stitch and branched fringe.

**37. Brenda Ford**
"The Ugly Duckling that Turned into a Beautiful Swan"   4.5 x 3 x .5 inches
Category: Body Adornment
Tubular and flat peyote, fringe embellishment, bead embroidery on cord.

**38. Robin A. Matthews**
"White Rabbit"   14 x 8.5 inches
Category: Wall Hanging
The "White Rabbit" was made using peyote stitch.

**39. Bent Needle Barb**
"The Dead Marshes"   17 x 15 inches
Category: Sculpture
Freeform peyote and netting were used to construct this piece.

## Native American

**40. Jan Zicarelli**
"Raven"   14.5 x 8.5 x 4 inches
Category: Sculpture
Stitches used include: brick stitch, peyote stitch, fringe and netting.

*41. Shgen George*
"Box of Daylight"   19 x 12 inches
Category: Wall Hanging
The beads were sewn onto a blue felt backing with two threads and one needle.

*42. Jacqué Owens*
"Creation and Ms. Turtle"   11.5 x 5 inches
Category: Sculpture
Stitches include: gourd stitch, one-, two-, and three-drop circular peyote and right-angle weave.

*43. Denise Palluck*
"Bag of Stars"   8 x 24 inches
Category: Sculpture
Three variations of peyote stitch were used: the picture is in flat single peyote the lid is done in circular flat peyote, and the bag is done in varying numbers of drop peyote.

*44. Francis "Casey" Case*
"Gifts of the Great Creator"   13 x 5 x 5 inches
Category: Sculpture
Tubular peyote was used for the body of the piece.
"Gifts of the Great Creator" is an illustration of the Native American folktale, **Song of the Seven Herbs** by Walking Night Bear.

*45. Kirsten Rugeley*
"Raven Steals the Sun"   2 x 3 inches
Category: Body Adornment
The bag was done in tubular odd count peyote stitch with tapered edges at top and bottom. The center sun ray, the bottom fringe tabs, the short blue and black tubes in the lower strap, and the upper neck strap were done in flat peyote stitch.

*46. Lisa Ann Claver*
"Quetzalcoatl"   13.5 x 13.5 cm
Category: Body Adornment
This piece was constructed with flat peyote, the arms were done with circular even count peyote and branched fringe.

*47. Jean Campbell*
"Dayo the Dead"   7 x 2 x 1 inches
Category: Sculpture
"Dayo the Dead" is made with sculptural peyote and is embellished with appliqué, fringe, and freeform sculptural techniques.

*48. Suzanne M. M. Warner*
"The Tobacco Society of the Crow Indians"   8 x 2.75 inches
Category: Body Adornment
This piece is done primarily in peyote stitch.

*49. Jennifer Fain*
"Medicine Bear Pouch"   24 x 2.5 inches
Category: Body Adornment
The body of the piece is done in flat peyote and brick stitch is used to attach the body to the strap.
The first set of beaded beads are made with circular peyote and closed with right-angle weave, and
the second set with netting.


## Fairy Tales

*50. JoAnn Feher*
"The Frog Prince"   4 x 2 x 1 inches
Category: Body Adornment
"The Frog Prince" is made in hollow, 3-dimensional peyote stitch.  It is freeform; there is no core.
The mask is papier maché with gold glitter and a twisted wire handle.

*51. Cary Franklin Gaspar*
"The Genie of the Lamp"   8 x 6 x 9.5 inches
Category: Sculpture
"The Genie of the Lamp" was constructed over a polymer clay and glass base using two-drop brick
stitch, right-angle weave, peyote stitch, Ndebele, and netting, with surface embellishment.

*52. Stella Broughton*
"A Fairy Tale"   5 x 6 inches
Category: Body Adornment
This piece was done using flat peyote stitch.


## The Phoenix and the Fire Bird

*53. Neva L. Wuerfel*
"Imminent Incineration"   20 x 19 x 19 inches
Category: Sculpture
This piece is made with peyote stitch with surface embellishment covering a heavy-gauge wire
wrapped in aluminum foil, then covered with polymer clay.

*54. Marian Crane*
"Phoenix in Flight"   7 x 15 inches
Category: Body Adornment
Stitches used include: flat and tubular peyote, right-angle weave, and fringe.

*55. Nancy Badciong*
"Russian Firebird"   14.5 x 16 x 1 inches
Category: Wall Hanging
Loom woven.

*56. Jill S. Cremer*
"Elvis, in the Guise of a Phoenix, Rises from the Ashes"
Category: Sculpture
Tubular peyote stitch and sculptural peyote was woven over a modeling compound armature to make "Elvis."

*57. Mary J. Winters-Meyer*
"Phoenix"   36 inches tall, 36 inches in circumference
Category: Sculpture
Stitches used include: tubular peyote, flat peyote, netting, linked chain stitch, looped fringe and brick stitch.

*58. Delphina*
"Phoenix Rising"   Headpiece : 9 x 6 inches, Necklace : 5 x 14 inches
Category: Body Adornment
Ladder and brick stitch were used to create the feathers, and the head and neck were formed with gourd stitch.

*59. Judy Walker*
"The Boy Who Drew Cats"   24 x 10 x 16 inches
Category: Sculpture
The four panels are loomed. The cat and rat were sculpted from taxidermist's foam and covered in variable-drop peyote stitch. Details are done in right-angle weave and brick stitch.


## Assorted Folk Tales, Myths and Legends

*60. Lynn Shansky*
"Vasilisa the Wise and Clever"   4.5 x 6 inches
Category: Wall Hanging
To construct the main portion of the piece the beads were embroidered upon the backing. Vasilisa's dress was made with freeform circular peyote.

*61. Amy C. Clarke*
"The Seven Swans: Moment of Transformation"    7.5 x 8 inches
Category: Wall Hanging
The piece was created using bead embroidery, working in a growing spiral from the center out.

*62. Maryalice W. Tomoeda*
"Momotaro"    3 x 18 inches
Category: Body Adornment
The pouch was woven with 2 x 2 right-angle weave with embellishment. The strap was done in square stitch using a variation on a Celtic wave pattern. Square stitch with embellishment was used for the banner. The amulets were made with baby wire.

*63. Wendy Ford*
"The Tortoise and the Hare (or Bad Hare Day)"    6 x 4.5 x 2.5 inches
Category: Sculpture
Somewhat circular peyote, increasing and decreasing, was used to give the moulded form of the shell "color shields." Between the color shields brick stitch was used. The edge of the shell was done in tubular brick stitch, and the inside of the box with the hare was made with flat peyote. (cont.) The inside and outside walls of the box were done in flat peyote with a few increases and decreases to make the fold-over more smooth. The underside of the box has peyote running perpendicularly to the peyote of the inside to give it more structural strength.

*64. Kerry Smith*
"The Emperor's Nightingale"    12 x 10 x 6 inches
Category: Sculpture
The nightingale was constructed using brick stitch, peyote stitch, and a simple joining stitch.

*65. Bonnie Bousquet-Smith*
"The Emperor and the Bird"    12 x 15 x 10 inches
Category: Sculpture
Stitches used include: peyote stitch (flat and tubular), brick stitch (flat and tubular), right-angle weave (flat and tubular), Nbedele or herringbone (flat and tubular), appliqué, chevron stitch, and the artist's own original stitch which forms the feathers and beak.

*66. Taeko Matoba*
"White Rabbit of Inaba"    108 x 30cm
Category: Sculpture
The four panels are woven.

*67. Kristin Tescher*
"Icarus"    59 x 10 inches
Category: Sculpture
Stitches used include: loom weaving, spiral rope technique, embroidery, twisted fringe, branched fringe, two-drop peyote and peyote ruffles.

### 68. Marla Kay Shelton
"Merlin's Book of Spells"   6.75 x 10 x 2.5 inches
Category: Sculpture
The base of the cover was loom woven, the snake head and tail are done in peyote stitch. The words are couched beads, and there is additional embroidery upon the cover.

### 69. Darlene Saric
"Green Man"   1 x 3 x 3.5 inches
Category: Wall Hanging
A molded silk paper mask was covered with beaded leaves partly attached to the mask and extended with peyote stitch. Other leaves were added over the base leaves.

### 70. Sue Maguire
"Grail"   5.5 x 3 inches
Category: Sculpture
"Grail" is worked entirely in tubular peyote stitch.

### 71. Linda Karel Sage
"Theseus, Ariadne, and the Minotaur"   6 x 6 inches
Category: Body Adornment
Square stitch was used to make the Minotaur, and the faces of Theseus and Ariadne were embedded as a mosaic on a Sculpey® base.

### 72. Susan R. Starkey
"The Celestial Unicorn"   8 x 10 inches
Category: Wall Hanging
The lady on the unicorn was outlined onto stiff white chair backing. I used bead embroidery to create this appliqué, which was then sewn onto velveteen. I also used bead embroidery to create the illusion of a flowing nighttime sky with stars.

### 73. Keiko Koyama
"Sagittarius"   22 x 42 centimeters.
Category: Wall Hanging
This piece is loom woven.

### 74. R.A. Hall
"Forever Ago: Under the Willow"   6 x 8 x 1 inches
Category: Body Adornment
Stitches used include: circular peyote, flat peyote, spike stitch, and surface embellishment.

### 75. Toni A. McMahon
"Pegasus Ascending to Olympus"  3.5 x 4.5 inches
Category: Body Adornment
Stitches used include flat, odd count, and freeform peyote stitch, with surface embellishments.

### 76. Marji Brohammer
"Cherubim Feathers"  7 x 2, 4 x .5, 4 x 1.75 inches
Category: Wall Hanging
The feathers are composed entirely of square stitch and variants of square stitch.

### 77. Susan Tucker
"The Hare in the Moon"  2.5 x 3 inches (total length with strap is 18 inches)
Category: Body Adornment
The body of the bag is made with even count tubular peyote, the bottom flap and side hinges are done with odd count flat peyote, and sculptural peyote is used to cover the bead in the tassel. The strap is bead crochet. The hare's footprints are depicted on the back of the bag.

### 78. Jean D. Barstow
"Luck Be a Ladybug"  2 x 3 inches (body)
Category: Body Adornment
Body: two brick stitched ivy leaves joined at the bottom and side edges. The neck chain consists of a brick stitched chain of red ladybugs with an additional chain of green branched fringe. Red white-heart beads accent the ladybug chain.


## Dragons

### 79. Brenda Whitehead
"The Guardian"  12.5 x 20.5 inches
Category: Sculpture
Peyote–flat, tubular, freeform, and netting–over wood and distressed iron.

### 80. Patsy Bruton
"Guardian of the Globe"  9 x 6 inches
Category: Sculpture
I worked forward from the tail using peyote, Comanche, and square stitches as well as some of my own. To maintain the true bead colors I used 4lb test fishing line. Legs and wings were created separately and added last. The dragon is stuffed with fiberfill and has a wire armature from tail to head which holds him to the globe. The globe was purchased from a glass blower in Ouray, CO.

*81. Vivien Exon*
"The Black Dragon of Peking"   11 x 15 inches
Category: Wall-hanging
Peyote stitch, even count, odd count and freeform brick stitch, spiral rope chain.

*82. Tery Baker*
"St. George's Dragon"   6.5 x 10.5 x 7.5 inches
Category: Sculpture
Over a substructure that I sculpted, a beadwork piece of flat peyote stitch was wrapped and secured. Beads were then stitched to the top and bottom of this piece in a modified brick stitch style until the entire dragon was covered with beads. The eyes are single beads sewn to the head. Eyelids, scales, wings, tail tip, and sword are either brick or freeform stitches.

*83. Christina Manes*
"Farouche"   12 x 14 inches
Category: Body Adornment
After many sketches, my entry started with a styrofoam wreath cut and glued to size. The form was then covered with papier maché. The skin was made with a combination of brick and peyote stitches. Larger beads helped create stretch points to curve the skin around the form. The body skin and face skin were done separately and then joined. Fringe was added last.

*84. Mary Lou Allen*
"Chinese Dragon"   21 x 5.5 inches
Category: Body Adornment
The main body of the piece is loom weaving done with Miyuki Delicas. A cinnabar medallion, cinnabar beads, and other black and brass beads are strung up one side and around the neck. The piece was finished without a clasp. The graduated levels of twisted fringe are accented by larger beads.

*85. Elida Cisneros*
"Rain Dragon"   Beaded center is 12 inches in diameter.
Category: Wall Hanging
Bead embroidery. The backing is cotton broadcloth on a layer of pellon.

*86. Jennifer Bumann*
"Dragon Purse"   4 x 6 inches not including tassel.
Category: Body Adornment
Designed on a Macintosh computer with Stitch Painter software, then hand embroidered on a cloth background. When finished I hand seamed all the edges and lined the purse with Chinese silk brocade.

*87. Jane Davis*
"Andvari's Treasure"    9.5 x 9 x 3 inches
Category: Sculpture
The cover of the box is couching and embroidery on silk. The top is a stranded technique of my own stitched on ultra suede. The front is peyote stitch appliquéd on silk and the interior is netting appliquéd onto silk. In addition to Miyuki Delicas I used a fossilized shark's tooth, antique steel cut beads, silver and gold-filled wire and beads, a variety of semiprecious stones, several findings, trim, etc.